Let Me Try It!

Enhancing maker education through digital fabrication

Dr. Tony Donen   Joshua Sneideman   Michael Stone

Let Me Try It!

by Dr. Tony Donen, Joshua Sneideman, and Michael Stone

Printed by CreateSpace, an Amazon.com company.

www.letmetryitbook.com

Cover and Illustration by Michael Stone

March 2018: First Edition

The authors have made every effort to ensure the accuracy of the information within this book was correct at time of publication. The authors do not assume and hereby disclaims any liability to any party for any loss, damage, or disruption caused by errors or omissions, whether such errors or omissions result from accident, negligence, or any other cause.

ISBN-13: 978-1986064880
ISBN-10: 1986064883

Contents

Introduction

Did you ever play dominoes when you were a kid, where you would set up lots of dominoes standing in curving S shape, then knock down the first domino to watch all the others fall in sequence? In 2012 a series of events helped set up the dominoes that led to Chattanooga, Tennessee becoming a world leader in digital fabrication education.

It began when Dr. Tony Donen was chosen to lead the first regional STEM school in Chattanooga, Tennessee. Tony and his staff were tasked with developing and implementing a student experience rooted in project and problem based learning where students would tackle real-world challenges that applied their learning.

Fast forward to August 2014. Michael Stone, a teacher at STEM School Chattanooga, led the development of the first Fab Lab in Tennessee, a digital fabrication space to help students turn ideas into realities. His efforts led to his selection as an Albert Einstein Distinguished Educator Fellow for the National Science Foundation where he worked in Washington D.C. helping support the CS for All initiative.

While a fellow at NSF, Michael met another Albert Einstein Distinguished Educator, Joshua Sneideman, who had recently moved to Chattanooga to take a leadership role at an education technology company, Learning Blade, working to inspire middle school students through stories of STEM careers. Josh, having finished writing two STEM books for Middle School educators, connected with Tony and Michael to share their educational insights in a joint collaboration.

In 2016, Michael chose to return to Chattanooga to lead the Public Education Foundation Office of Innovative Learning. As part of his work, Michael was tasked with helping develop and implement a plan to bring digital fabrication to public schools in Hamilton County. In partnership with the Volkswagen Group of America, Chattanooga Operations (Volkswagen Chattanooga), Public Education Foundation, Hamilton County Department of Education (HCDE) and the State of Tennessee, Michael began working on the establishment of 16 proposed digital fabrication labs in middle schools and high schools. Dubbed "Volkswagen eLabs," the program provides students access to emergent technologies, including automated manufacturing equipment, 3D printers, robotics, microcomputers, renewable energy kits, and digital design tools.

August 2017, based off the STEM School Fab Lab model, the first eight state-of-the-art digital fabrication laboratories opened in public middle schools and high schools in the Chattanooga area. Following a summer of facilities retrofitting and 112 hours of professional development, full time teachers identified as VW eLab Specialists were empowered to establish and successfully embed digital fabrication in traditional public schools.

January 2018, STEM School Chattanooga was selected as one of two schools in the world to take part in a leadership cohort for digital fabrication education because of the successful implementation of its Fab Lab initiatives. By this time, STEM School Chattanooga was recognized as a global incubator for educational innovations and had emerged as a leader in pioneering innovative practices in education. The school was visited by thousands of educators from across the globe, impacting the learning of tens of thousands of students.

Today, Chattanooga is demonstrating how to scale this innovative work by successfully integrating digital fabrication labs in 18 public schools serving a diverse range of students in traditional settings. Want to learn more about digital fabrication and how we might help you bring it to your population? Visit www.letmetryitbook.com

The following pages are designed to inspire and provide practical advice on leveraging digital fabrication to impact education. Chapters 1-7 make a case for digital fabrication in education while chapters 8-14 provide the steps for implementation.

Welcome to the world of digital fabrication and rich learning experiences!

Sincerely,
Tony, Joshua, Michael

Let Me Try It!

Enhancing maker education
through digital fabrication

Let Me Try It!

You download a new game to your phone and a 5-year old sees you playing it. You know what phrase will be excitedly uttered next, "Lemme try it! I want a turn. Can I please just have one turn? I just want to try it." Kids love to engage. They crave opportunities to "try it." What would school look like if students came to class with that same level of excitement and anticipation? They will, but we have to shift how we approach teaching, learning, and assessing to develop that energizing atmosphere.

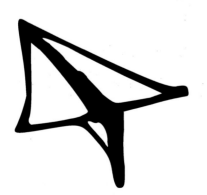

- Students want to learn in dynamic, experiential settings.
- If I can't experience it, I can't internalize it.
- Contextually relevant work delivers high level learning opportunities.

Students from kindergarten through higher-ed want to engage in exploration and authentic problem solving. They want to "try it!" As we transition out of the information age and into the conceptual age, it is clear that students, now more than ever, desire and deserve opportunities to engage, explore, experience, and create. In a media and information saturated world, it is critical that teachers cultivate learning environments that give students opportunities to experience learning in authentic and relevant contexts. Innovative educators are embracing digital fabrication as the vehicle to do just that!

Give the pupils something to do, not something to learn; and the doing is of such a nature as to demand thinking; learning naturally results.
-- John Dewey

Stop Consuming...Start Creating!

My three daughters remind me that I constantly live in a microcosm of society. I will walk into the living room of my house and be immediately hit with the following situation — one daughter watching a show on an iPad, another daughter searching for YouTube videos about the newest fad, and the third daughter playing a Barbie DVD. This situation often also leads to the inevitable statement by one or more of my daughters, "Dad, I'm bored". But that is not always how I am greeted. There was the day I went downstairs to find my entire living room transformed into a maze with all three girls yelling, "Dad, you gotta try out what we made!" Or the day I heard chanting, "Dad, Dad, Dad, come here!" I found all 3 daughters standing over a tower of princesses and Legos with each girl explaining how this part didn't work, but then they made different changes and now we have the 8th wonder of the world. I know this... life is drastically different when my girls are creators and not just consumers.

Stages of Creating

Create Here!

Create   Create something entirely new

Modify   Take what others have done; modify it into something new

Embellish   Add something to that which has been done

Hone   Keep copying multiple examples to refine your skills

Copy   Make something almost exactly as someone else has done

We live in a world where kids (and adults) are programmed constantly to be consumers. We are told what to like, what to think, and what to be. We are told what is right and what is wrong, and we learn to be compliant to whatever it is we have chosen to be the focal point of our consumption. We know that consumption can provide fleeting periods of joy. On the other hand, true joy, passion, personalization, and meaningfulness are the result of creation. By definition, creating is simply the act of making something. The common argument made by educators that misunderstand the role of creating in education is that it is not found in the standardized curriculum. That's not because creating is not vital to student growth, it is because it is an action—not a thing. Creating is the process by which you develop student skills through the act of making. Creating is not in opposition to standardized curriculum. Creating is the lever to bring the standardized curriculum to life. We need students who are as adept at creating as they are at consuming. In that world, we are part of a highly productive, purposeful, and passionate community.

There is no truer moment of being oneself than in the moment when we are making our ideas come to life.
- Dr. Tony Donen

Learn and Do

You have an amazing idea for a project the students can do. However, you realize that after you introduce the unit, teach the concepts in the unit, grade homework, give a few quizzes and finish with a cumulative test, there is no time for the students to do the project. Maybe somehow next year.

Projects in making are not intended to be elaborate tasks that students do "after" the learning has already taken place. They shouldn't be dessert. Rather, maker projects are best exemplified by their connection with PBL (project/problem based learning) where the learning happens alongside the making.

Making can happen when...

- **Time is more flexible.** In these cases, students can dive into Design Challenges. Design Challenges provide students with the opportunity to apply content already learned or tackle problems that are content agnostic.

- **Making is embedded.** Making is a tremendous opportunity to embed learning throughout a unit and create a need to learn content for students. PBL units implemented well are great allies with making.

So you're saying the learning happens IN the creating!

PBL can be great. PBL integrated with making is legendary. And legends are what we remember.

— Dr. Tony Donen

Where Content Meets Process
understanding what really matters

You were asked by your boss to interview candidates for a professional job and here is what took place:

Applicant #1
Top of his class, recited an immeasurable number of facts, but questioned nothing.

Applicant #2
Great personality, was very smooth, but content information she presented and explained had errors.

Applicant #3
Provided examples of innovative project ideas, collaborative work, and asked thoughtful questions.

You recommended #3... but why?

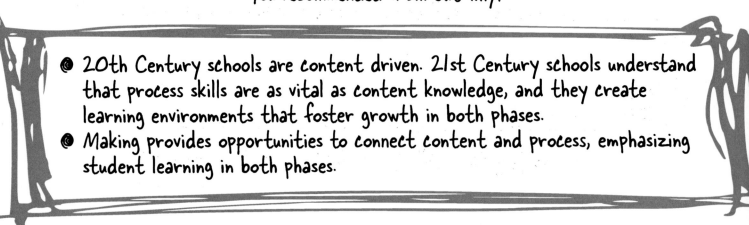

- 20th Century schools are content driven. 21st Century schools understand that process skills are as vital as content knowledge, and they create learning environments that foster growth in both phases.
- Making provides opportunities to connect content and process, emphasizing student learning in both phases.

In 2010, it was estimated that we created as much information in 2 days than what was created up until 2003. Around the same time Wolfram Alpha, a computational knowledge engine (or simply answer key to everything) was launched. We no longer live in a world that is dependent on looking for a person with all the content knowledge. We live in a world that needs people to find knowledge, decipher it, then use and apply it.

Schools that only focus on content acquisition are already outdated. Processes (like critical thinking, innovation, collaboration, etc.) are as important, if not more, to the future success of our students. The successful schools of the next generation will be focused on processes as much as content. Making provides an avenue to connect content and process together so our students are really ready to challenge applicant #3.

Knowing googleable facts won't get you very far in today's world, making something meaningful with them will.
                                                    -Dr. Tony Donen

Making for All

The gender, socioeconomic, and ethnicity gaps in STEM are pervasive and well documented. Many speculate that the gap is due entirely to a lack of awareness of the vast opportunities in emerging STEM fields. However, exposing students to STEM workforce needs is only part of the solution. The critical piece of the puzzle lies in contextual relevance and personalization for each student.

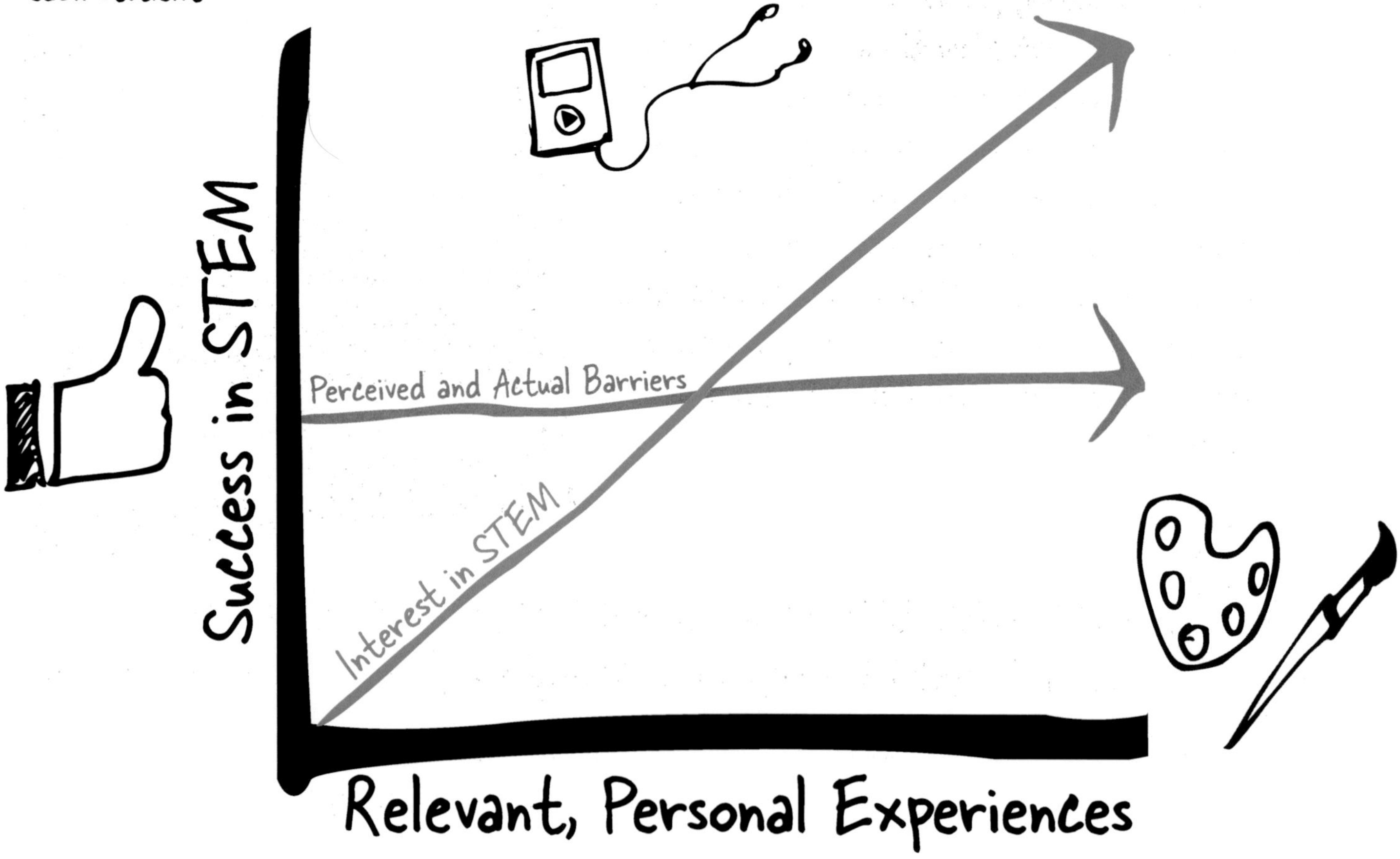

Success in STEM

Perceived and Actual Barriers

Interest in STEM

Relevant, Personal Experiences

Empower students to overcome barriers (apathy, fear, accessibility, perceived lack of ability) by:
- wrapping learning experiences in contextually relevant problems
- providing access to digital fabrication tools that enable rapid prototyping
- incentivizing students to explore creative solutions to real problems
- exposing students to diverse role models in the field

Students who engage in authentic making in the context of problem solving, are empowered to explore creative solutions that align with their unique interests. When students engage in solving problems they care about, with access to tools that allow them to make functional solutions with a minimal learning curve, their intrinsic motivation to master the skills necessary to solve the problems empowers them to overcome STEM barriers. When repeated, this exposure results in all students developing self confidence in their ability to succeed in emergent fields as they discover how they can personally contribute in a way that aligns with their personality, aptitudes, and interests.

Children learn best when they are actively constructing something that has personal meaning to them -- be it a poem, a robot, a sandcastle, or a computer program.

~ Seymour Papert

Master Learners

Digital fabrication presents students with opportunities to discover novel solutions to problems of personal interest. In the process, they not only develop a deeper understanding of content that is anchored to contextually relevant problem solving, they also refine process skills that empower them to effectively manage their projects. This holistic approach to learning provides students with richer, more meaningful, and transferable learning experiences.

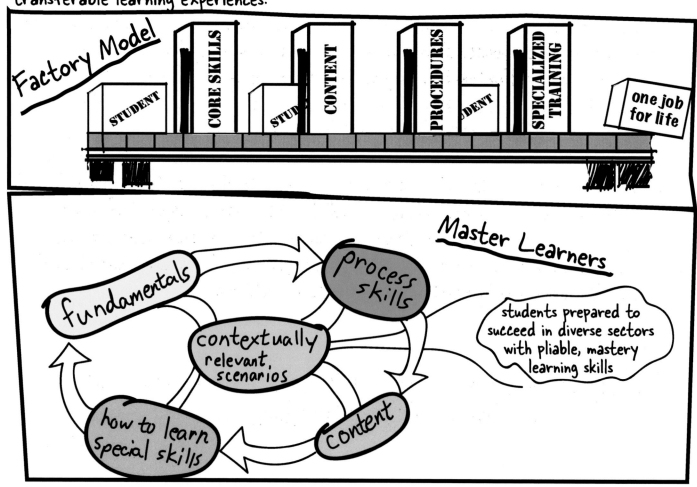

Master Learners:

- are empowered to model their learning
- demonstrate that not knowing is OK
- are confident because of their resourcefulness
- are excellent at asking meaningful questions
- effectively evaluate new information for accuracy and applicability
- are flexible and can confidently adapt to situations requiring new skills

In recent years, the idea of enabling students to thrive as experts has become popular rhetoric, but very few practical options are offered to actually facilitate deep learning for students. Fortunately, digital fabrication serves as an excellent conduit to empower students as experts without minimizing the role of the teacher. Rather than reducing the value of the teacher's role, digital fabrication increases each student's role by fostering ownership over their own learning, while shifting the teacher's role to that of master learner. Through this lens, every person in the experience, students and teachers alike, becomes an independent and collaborative learner capable of identifying, analyzing, and sharing information throughout an organic experience. This not only results in students having a more robust learning experience, it also empowers students to develop the adaptability required in the modern workforce.

It's not about what you know. It's about how quickly you can learn and apply something new.

--Michael Stone

Simplifying the

You are in your fifth professional development session of the week and the entire session is devoted to learning more about Bloom's Taxonomy. This is the 23rd time you have been in some sort of class about Bloom's. The session leader does as good or better than anyone else you have seen, and you leave with a spinning wheel that defines all six levels of Bloom's, and each of the levels includes three teacher "to-do's", 13 different ways you can ask questions, and has 42 different verbs that are considered "power" words. In total, you have 354 new combinations to define Bloom's Taxonomy. Later the next week, you put the new items and the spinning wheel of Bloom's Taxonomy on your bookshelf to reference sometime the next year... maybe.

For many years, schools have been focused on trying to ensure that all students can learn and that teachers have a plethora of insights into the varying levels of Bloom's. But the reality is that many teacher developed lessons support strong learning of the first two levels of Bloom's Taxonomy only — knowledge and understanding. How then can we realistically make sure that all students learn at the higher levels of Bloom's Taxonomy? Simply put, through making and digital fabrication. Making simplifies the higher levels of Bloom's by creating a tangible, realistic, and clear path for all kids to learn at higher levels. Digital fabrication empowers students to engage in functional making leveraging rapid prototyping tools.

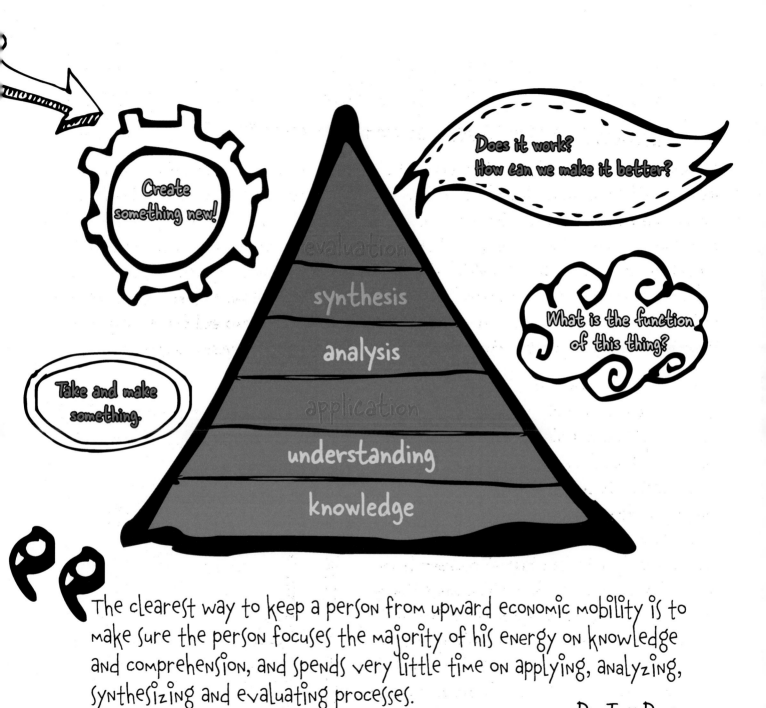

The clearest way to keep a person from upward economic mobility is to make sure the person focuses the majority of his energy on knowledge and comprehension, and spends very little time on applying, analyzing, synthesizing and evaluating processes.

-Dr. Tony Donen

14

Let's Create!

Your daughter just turned four years old and you decide it's time for her to learn how to ride a bicycle. You both head outside to get started, and you sit her on the bicycle. As you look at the bike and at her, you realize you have no idea how to explain to her how to do this. You begin walking around thinking to yourself, "How can I explain balance to a four year old let alone the fact that velocity helps establish and maintain that balance?" As you begin to worry that you are going to be the one parent who can't figure this out, you look back at your daughter and she is pushing herself around the driveway. She has already figured out how to use her feet to act as a balance and create momentum. Within three days, she has figured out how to push herself the entire way across the driveway and put her feet in the air between pushes. Within a week, she has figured out how to push herself and put her feet on the pedals, and has even begun to turn. And, finally, within two weeks, she is pedaling. A month after that first day where you worried you might be the worst parent ever, she somehow has figured this whole thing out and is yelling to you, "Daddy, watch me ride around the driveway!"

Start Here

Before you start making for the first time, there is a constant fear that you are just not ready. You need to know more. Someone needs to show you how to do this. There is a right way and procedures and protocols and a list of instructions... right? Yes and no. There is always training that can take place, but creating, in its essence, is not googleable. It is a learning experience. When embedded in authentic making, learning is accentuated through experience, failures, ideation, and varied applications. Like the first time on a bike, in maker education, you just have to go for it!

Getting started in making and not sure where to start? Here are some basic steps:

- Sketch what you want to make.
- Figure out the most basic materials you can use to build a rough prototype of your sketch (cardboard is always a favorite!)
- Decide what equipment/tools you need to make your rough prototype (learn how to use the equipment/tool if you do not have familiarity already... that is googleable)
- Build the rough prototype
- Make adjustments in design
- Repeat as many times as necessary scaling up materials, equipment, tools, and complexity of design.

The successful people are not stagnant, they are iterative and they cannot be iterative until they start.

-Dr. Tony Donen

Where Iteration Meets Quality

In one of my classes, we tasked two groups with creating a projectile to fly as far as possible. On presentation day in front of college professors from the local university, two of the teams had drastically different presentations and results.

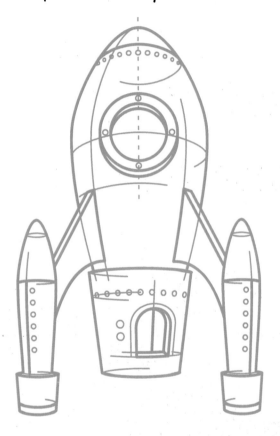

Team A shot their projectile about 25 yards (furthest in the class) and the team explained how they had built this projectile on their 1st attempt. Team F shot their projectile and it literally went 0.0 yards, hit the ground and shattered. Team F explained the 13 iterations of their projectile in their presentation, even showing where earlier projectiles had been more successful but the team wanted to see if they could keep making the prototype better. After all teams finished, the professors conferred and pronounced the winning team... Team F. All of the students were in shock and confused. The professors explained that the learning demonstrated in Team F's iterative work was far and away the best they had seen in years. If only every team was as impressive.

Students are led to believe that the only item that matters is the final product. Yet learning is not only about the end result, true learning is about the entire process. Making provides an avenue to transform student thinking to focus on process rather than result. In the above example, yes, a final result of a non-flying projectile is not optimal. But the learning that occurred as a result of Team F's willingness to iterate through failure was remarkable. Ultimately, students need to value learning (& the process) as much, if not more than, the result.

When you want to value learning through failure:

- Explain to students that the end result is not the only component being judged, but so is the process by which the students attained the end result.

- Have students explain the making process they went through, not just their final product.

- Let students present a timeline of the process used for their product.

- Require students to iterate multiple times, having students identify the positives of each iteration and the areas to strengthen for the next iterations.

The 13th iteration (before it shattered) →

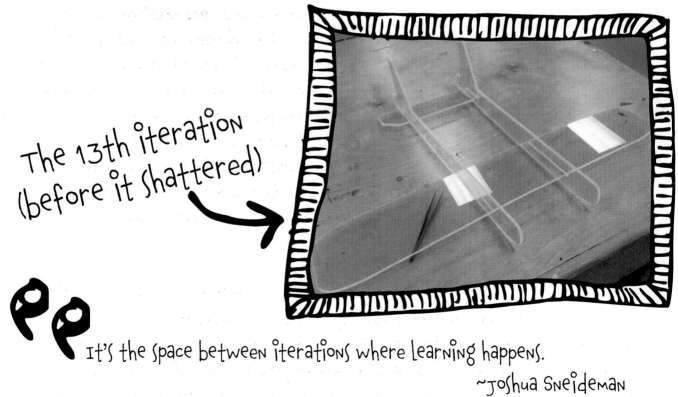

It's the space between iterations where learning happens.

~Joshua Sneideman

The Right Stuff?

Conceptually, the starting point to making is simply starting. It's making the decision to jump in—to embrace the risk of trying something new because of the incredible potential it has for your students. However, digital fabrication, is a little more complicated. Everyone operates on a budget and purchasing technology, especially digital fabrication technology, can quickly become overwhelming. But there is good news! A little insight can make this process much more manageable.

You are embracing the digital fabrication movement and are excited to build your school's digital fabrication lab. What do you buy? Where do you start? If you lack specific expertise, a quality consultant can provide critical guidance to help you make informed choices. Before you jump off the deep end, please consider most people learn to hammer before they learn to laser cut. Allow your digital fabrication lab to follow a similar arc. Sure there are the overnight grant winners who go from zero to hero with a shiny new million dollar lab. Or maybe you've heard stories of $100,000 grants to build a brand new lab at a neighboring high school. These stories are great, but there are a variety of entry points. No matter where you begin, once you demonstrate the proof of concept--that digital fabrication drastically changes how we think about teaching and learning--more opportunities will come!

The equipment in a digital fabrication lab should vary by grade levels served as well as by school community needs. However, as a rough starting point, consider the following:

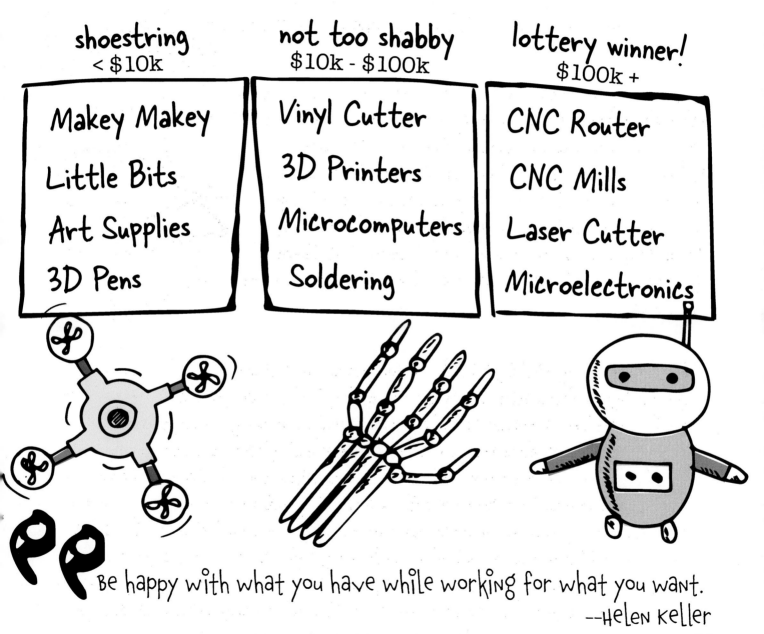

shoestring < $10k	not too shabby $10k - $100k	lottery winner! $100k +
Makey Makey	Vinyl Cutter	CNC Router
Little Bits	3D Printers	CNC Mills
Art Supplies	Microcomputers	Laser Cutter
3D Pens	Soldering	Microelectronics

Be happy with what you have while working for what you want.
--Helen Keller

Partnerships That Matter

You attend a luncheon of the local chamber of commerce and the speaker gets up to talk about the state of education in your district. The speaker talks about how there is a desperate need for workplace ready employees and talks about the gap between the number of students coming out of school and the number of applicants who are hireable. By the time the speaker is finished, the business and community people in the audience are nodding passionately in agreement with the speaker. Post speech, no one has a solution, and even worse, the conversation turns into degrading the local school system. Every part of you wants to defend the schools, but you know that won't change any opinions. You attended the luncheon in hopes of asking for some more money to help your school, but even you are now wondering if that will solve any long term problems.

Workplace Ready
Student

Tips for Business and Education Partnerships:

- Don't ask a business for money or a speaker for career day. Ask a business partner to spend 30-60 minutes with an educator (or group of educators) to create a making project that is meaningful to the business community.
- Have the business partner kick-off a making project with the students and provide the students with background information on why the making project is important to the business partner.
- Set up a project presentation and feedback opportunity for the business partner to hear students present and showcase their making project. Have business partner provide student teams with both positive and constructive feedback. This small gesture lets students know people outside the walls of the school care about their work.

The schoolhouse and the business community have been separated into mutually exclusive entities. Education has been left to the educators, the experts in instruction of state required content. However, businesses have been left on the outside looking in with little influence as to the content, and no other resource except to point fingers. Except it does not have to be that way. Making provides the opportunity for businesses to "have skin in the game" and work collaboratively with educators in developing worthwhile, meaningful work. When students work on problems and issues that matter to them, they take ownership over their work which produces higher quality results and richer learning experiences.

> The best learning communities are those where businesses partner with educators in creating projects for students such that the work is real, timely and meaningful.
>
> -Dr. Tony Donen

Entrepreneurism
identify problems -- create solutions

You love lemonade and your five year old does as well. What happens next? The same thing that happens across every neighborhood in America, your five year old opens the street corner lemonade stand. Entrepreneurism happens early in life. Why do schools abandon teaching entrepreneurism?

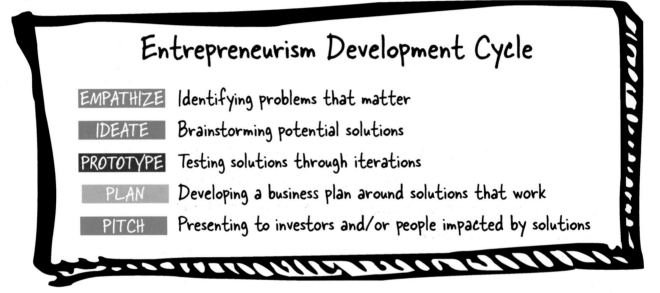

Entrepreneurism Development Cycle

EMPATHIZE	Identifying problems that matter
IDEATE	Brainstorming potential solutions
PROTOTYPE	Testing solutions through iterations
PLAN	Developing a business plan around solutions that work
PITCH	Presenting to investors and/or people impacted by solutions

Entrepreneurism is not a skill we teach in school. The reality is that it requires a student to not only be a problem solver who can apply, analyze, synthesize and evaluate information, but it also requires a skill we rarely teach – problem identification. Making leads us to the natural precipice where students tell us that they don't want us to tell them the problem to solve anymore, they want to identify it. This is truly transformational. Self-actualization occurs when they can identify meaningful problems to solve, brainstorm solutions, iteratively test their solutions, and bring their solutions to market. In other words, self-actualization occurs when students become entrepreneurial thinkers.

Provide students with a trivial problem, define the content they should use

Provide students with a meaningful problem, define the content they should use

Provide students with multiple meaningful problems, they pick problem and the best strategy to solve it

Students identify a problem to solve and solutions demonstrate how to solve it

Studentpreneur Progression

The entrepreneurial spirit is born within us. Providing students with avenues to let this spirit blossom separates the good learning from the great.

-Dr. Tony Donen

Network of Makers

Professional growth doesn't happen in a vacuum. Sure we can teach ourselves new skills, habits and approaches, but to truly reach our potential as educators we benefit from the experiences, successes and failures of others. We benefit from sharing our own examples and receiving feedback from other professionals. Similarly in the process of providing feedback to others we become a part of a network. The innovative shared experiences digital fabrication ushers in result in a thriving network of like-minded individuals and groups who are eager to learn and grow together!

Fab Foundation
fabfoundation.org

The US based non-profit that emerged from MIT is the preeminent authority on Fab Labs.

Maker Media
makermedia.com

Maker movement authority working to empower makers around the world.

Remake Learning
remakelearning.org

Network that ignites and champions strategies to embed "learning by doing."

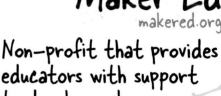

Maker Ed
makered.org

Non-profit that provides educators with support to develop maker-centered education a reality.

VW eLabs
vwelab.org

Exemplar of how to scale digital fabrication into traditional public schools

If you want to go fast, go alone. If you want to go far, go with others.

~ African Proverb

Coming Full Circle

You are now ready to engage in digital fabrication. You feel like there is something missing though. You can't put your finger on it, but you just can't shake the feeling. In the preceding pages you learned how to get started. Now you want to be a true master. What's next?

Making & digital fabrication are a process. There are a lot of resources already available to makers for learning about process cycles like continuous improvement, design thinking, the engineering design cycle, and others. Whether in a low-tech maker space or a full digital fabrication lab, teachers can develop their craft by embracing process cycles and learning how to apply them in classroom experiences with students. We have shared some of our favorites with you here:

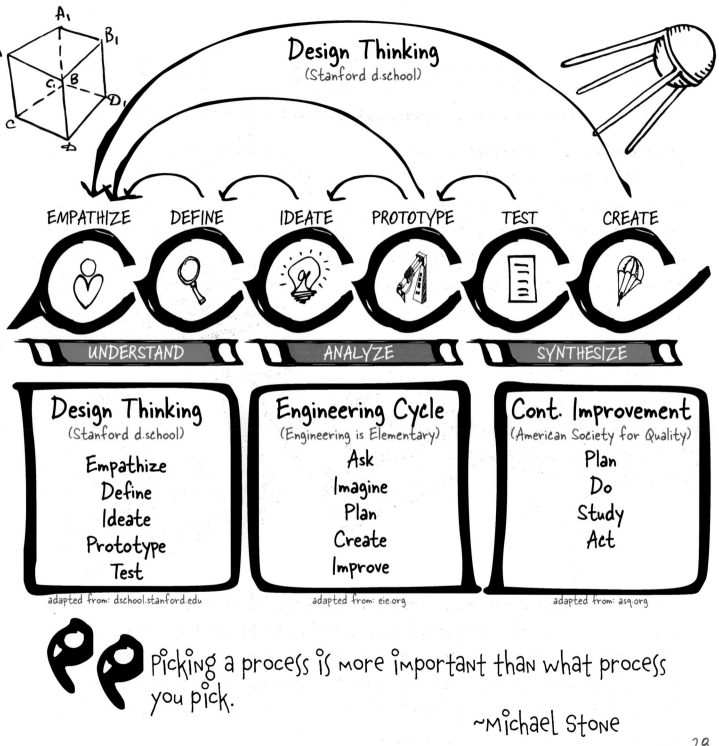

Design Thinking
(Stanford d.school)

EMPATHIZE   DEFINE   IDEATE   PROTOTYPE   TEST   CREATE

UNDERSTAND   ANALYZE   SYNTHESIZE

Design Thinking
(Stanford d.school)

Empathize
Define
Ideate
Prototype
Test

adapted from: dschool.stanford.edu

Engineering Cycle
(Engineering is Elementary)

Ask
Imagine
Plan
Create
Improve

adapted from: eie.org

Cont. Improvement
(American Society for Quality)

Plan
Do
Study
Act

adapted from: asq.org

Picking a process is more important than what process you pick.

~Michael Stone

28

Special Thanks

Tony, Joshua, and Michael would like to give special thanks and recognition to our wives and our collective 9 daughters, whose love and devotion motivate us to strive each and every day.

Follow the authors on Twitter

Tony @tonydonen   Michael @CoachStone12   Josh @STEMAGOGY

Share a digital copy with your friends and colleagues!
www.letmetryitbook.com

For professional development, speaking engagements, or digital fabrication consulting, please contact us at info@devxpd.org

"The role of the teacher is to create the conditions for invention rather than provide ready-made knowledge"

~Dr. Seymour Papert

Made in the USA
Middletown, DE
21 May 2018